EXAMINING POND HABITATS

Zelda King

PowerKiDS press.
New York

Published in 2009 by The Rosen Publishing Group, Inc.
29 East 21st Street, New York, NY 10010

First Edition

Editor: Joanne Randolph
Book Design: Kate Laczynski
Photo Researcher: Jessica Gerweck

Photo Credits: Cover, p. 1 © Steven Wooster/Getty Images; pp. 5, 7 (mountain pond, meadow pond, farm pond), 11 (cattails, wildflowers, water lilies, duckweed), 15, 19, 21 (water lily) Shutterstock.com; p. 7 (kettle pond) © Yva Momatiuk/John Eastcott/Getty Images, Inc.; p. 9 © Neil Fletcher & Matthew Ward/Getty Images; p. 13 (All Images) © Clip Art; p. 17 (frog) © www.istockphoto.com/Jozsef Szasz-Fabian; p. 17 (eggs) © www.istockphoto.com/Darcy Stuart; p. 17 (tadpole) © www.istockphoto.com/Thomas Mounsey; p. 17 (frog with legs) © www.istockphoto.com/Ron Brancato; p. 17 (froglet) © www.istockphoto.com/Morley Read; p. 21 (raccoon) © www.istockphoto.com/Frank Leung; p. 21 (toad) © www.istockphoto.com/John Bell; p. 21 (snail) © www.istockphoto.com/Laurie Knight.

Library of Congress Cataloging-in-Publication Data

King, Zelda.
  Examining pond habitats / Zelda King. — 1st ed.
      p. cm. — (Graphic organizers. Habitats)
  Includes index.
  ISBN 978-1-4358-2717-2 (library binding) — ISBN 978-1-4358-3121-6 (pbk.)
ISBN 978-1-4358-3127-8 (6-pack)
  1. Pond ecology—Juvenile literature. 2. Ponds—Juvenile literature. 3. Habitat (Ecology)—Juvenile literature.
I. Title.
  QH541.5.P63K56 2009
  577.63'6—dc22

                         2008023409

Manufactured in the United States of America

CONTENTS

WHAT IS A POND HABITAT?

Habitats are everywhere. They are the different places where plants and animals live, such as a desert or forest. A pond is a habitat, too. A pond is a little bit like a lake. A pond is small, quiet, and not very deep, though. A lake is larger and deeper than a pond.

A pond habitat is full of life. Graphic organizers can help you learn about it. A Venn diagram, for example, makes it easy to see how pond and lake habitats are alike and different. Use this book's graphic organizers to learn cool facts about a pond habitat!

Ponds are home to many plants and animals. A group of ducks swims in this pond, looking for food to eat.

ALL SORTS OF PONDS

A pond is a pond, right? Not really. Ponds are sorted into many types based on how or where they form. **Glaciers** high up in the mountains form mountain ponds. These ponds generally have ice in them and dry up in summer.

Glaciers form kettle ponds, too. Kettles are holes left behind when a glacier melts. If these holes fill with water, are small, and are not fed by rivers, they are called kettle ponds.

Meadow-stream ponds form where streams slow down and spread out. Altogether, there are more than 10 types of ponds!

This comparison chart shows us how different kinds of ponds are alike and different. Use the chart to find out if there are any features that all ponds share.

Comparison Chart: Comparing Pond Types

	Mountain Pond	Meadow-Stream Pond	Farm Pond	Kettle Pond
Formed by a glacier	X			X
Formed by a stream		X		
Human-made			X	
Formed high in mountains	X			X
Found in meadows		X	X	X
Found on farms		X	X	X
Stones on bottom	X			X
Muddy bottom	X	X	X	X
Ice in it	X			
Dries up in summer	X			
Many plants and animals	X	X	X	X
Good for swimming			X	X
Supplies water for crops, cows, and horses			X	

PLENTY OF PLANTS

Plants love ponds! Why do you think that is? Plants need water to live, and a pond gives a lasting supply. That is why you will find so many plants growing in and around ponds.

Many types of trees and bushes grow near ponds. You might see trees, such as maples, willows, pines, and cedars. You might see bushes that have flowers and berries, such as hawthorn, dogwood, and honeysuckle.

Short and tall grasses grow near ponds, too. You will also find small plants with flowers, such as St. John's wort, and many kinds of wildflowers.

This fishbone map gives us facts about the parts of a plant that grows near ponds. The blue lines tell us the parts, and the smaller lines tell us more about each part.

Fishbone Map: Parts of a Flowering Pond Plant

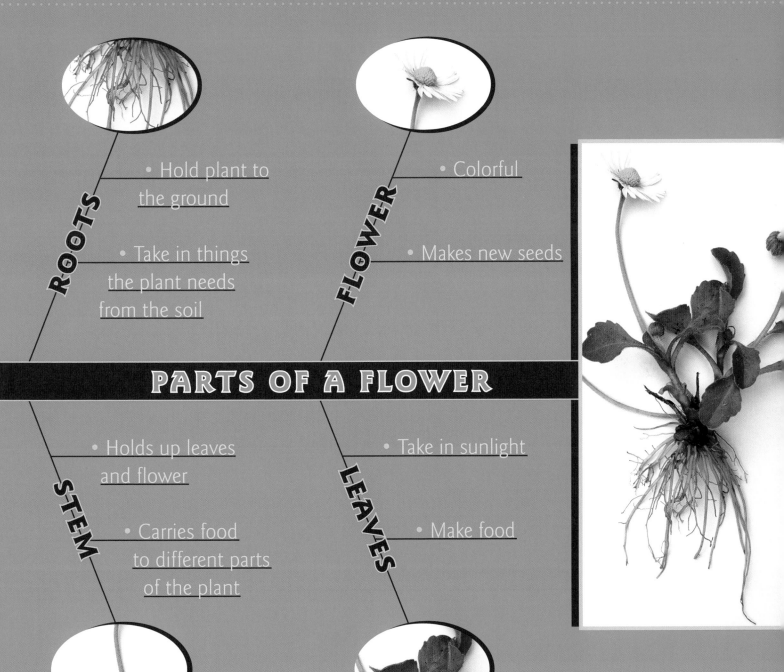

ROOTS
- Hold plant to the ground
- Take in things the plant needs from the soil

FLOWER
- Colorful
- Makes new seeds

PARTS OF A FLOWER

STEM
- Holds up leaves and flower
- Carries food to different parts of the plant

LEAVES
- Take in sunlight
- Make food

PLANTS IN THE WATER

Lots of plants grow near ponds. Did you know that many plants grow in ponds, though? Plants growing close to the edges have their roots in the pond's bottom. Their stems, leaves, and flowers emerge from, or stick up above, the water. These plants are called emergent plants.

Farther out in the pond are floating plants. Some have roots growing in the pond's bottom. Others can float anywhere because their roots just hang in the water. Very tiny plants called **phytoplankton** also float in the pond.

Some plants grow totally under the water, too! They are called **submersed** plants.

A star diagram can be a good way to list different ideas that relate to a main idea. This one tells us some of the different water plants in ponds.

ANIMALS AROUND A POND

All sorts of land animals make their homes in a pond habitat. It supplies them with food and water. Some even begin their lives in the water.

Deer drink from the pond and eat land plants. Beavers build homes in ponds and eat land and water plants. Raccoons, ducks, geese, and swans visit ponds.

There are many smaller animals as well. Frogs, toads, and many **insects** begin their lives in ponds and live nearby after they are grown. Turtles, snakes, rats, salamanders, worms, and spiders can also be found. Everywhere you look, you find animals around a pond!

A classifying web is a great way to sort ideas and facts. Can you use this chart to help you name some animals that live in a pond habitat?

Classifying Web: Pond Land Animals

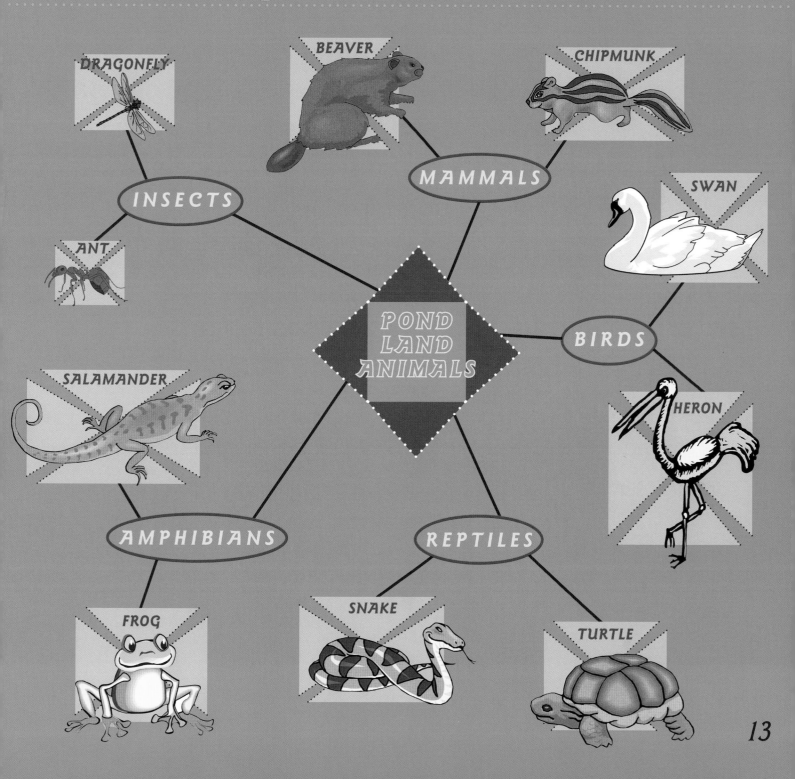

THE WATER IS WILD!

If you peer into a pond, you will see that it is full of animals. There are big fish and little fish. There may be **crustaceans**, such as shrimp and crayfish, as well. Some kinds of turtles spend their lives in the water.

If you lift the leaf of a floating plant, you may find snails. You may also find the eggs and young of some types of insects, such as dragonflies and mosquitoes. Frog and toad eggs and **tadpoles** are in the pond, too.

A pond also has animals called **zooplankton**. These animals are so tiny that you cannot see them!

This spider map lists four things about a crayfish and gives two details for each of those four things. Can you create your own map about another pond animal?

Spider Map: The Crayfish

BODY

Three parts

Hard outer covering

LEGS

Five pairs

One set of claws, four pairs of legs for walking

CRAYFISH

FOOD

Many kinds of plants

Small animals such as snails, tadpoles, small fish

EATEN BY

Some large fish

People

A CLOSER LOOK:
A FROG'S LIFE CYCLE

Many plants and animals call ponds home. Frogs are special because they live part of their lives in the water of the pond and part on land.

A frog begins its **life cycle** as an egg. A mother frog lays eggs in the pond. After a few days, tadpoles come out of the eggs. The tadpoles have long tails and no legs. They look like little fish and breathe through **gills**. Slowly, the tadpoles grow legs and **lungs**. Finally, the tadpoles lose their gills and tails and hop onto land as adult frogs. Soon, the cycle will begin again.

Cycle organizers are one way of showing something that happens over and over again. In this cycle chart, we see the stages, or steps, in a frog's life.

Cycle Organizer: Life Cycle of a Frog

A mother frog lays a lot of tiny eggs in the water.

The eggs hatch and a tadpole comes out of each egg. The tadpole has gills and a tail.

An adult frog has no tail and breathes with lungs. The frog is ready to mate and lay eggs of its own. Ribbit!

Soon, the tadpole becomes a froglet. It breathes with lungs and its tail is starting to grow smaller.

Next, the tadpole grows bigger and grows legs. It still breathes with gills and has a tail.

ONE BIG COMMUNITY

The people where you live form a community, right? Well, the plants and animals in a pond habitat form a community, too. They all play a part in keeping the community healthy.

All members of the community have a job. The plants are food for many animals and put **oxygen** in the water for pond animals to breathe. Animals that eat plants are food for other animals.

If there are too many or too few of one member of the community, it can change life for all. Some groups may disappear from the community.

Concept webs show how certain ideas or facts are connected to each other. Can you see how each piece of the pond habitat is important to keep the pond community in balance?

Concept Web: The Need for Balance

Pond Community

land plants

land animals

water plants

water animals

supply oxygen and food

some eat plants, some eat animals

too many of one kind can crowd out others

too few plant-eating animals means too many plants and not enough food for animal-eating animals

too few animal-eating animals means there will be too many plant-eating animals

too few means not enough food for animals

too many plant-eating animals will eat too many plants

habitat out of balance

19

A POND FOOD CHAIN

Do you know what a food chain is? Each member in the food chain eats the one before it. This might not sound nice, but it keeps the pond community in balance.

Food chains start with plants. That is because plants make their own food from sunlight, air, and water. Next in the chain are animals that eat plants. Then come animals that eat plant-eating animals and perhaps plants as well. Next in the chain are those animals that eat the smaller meat-eating animals. Those animals may, in turn, be eaten by other, larger animals.

This pyramid chart shows some of the animals at each level of the pond food chain. The photos show one possible chain, starting with a raccoon eating a toad, the toad eating a snail, and so on.

Pyramid Chart: A Pond Food Chain

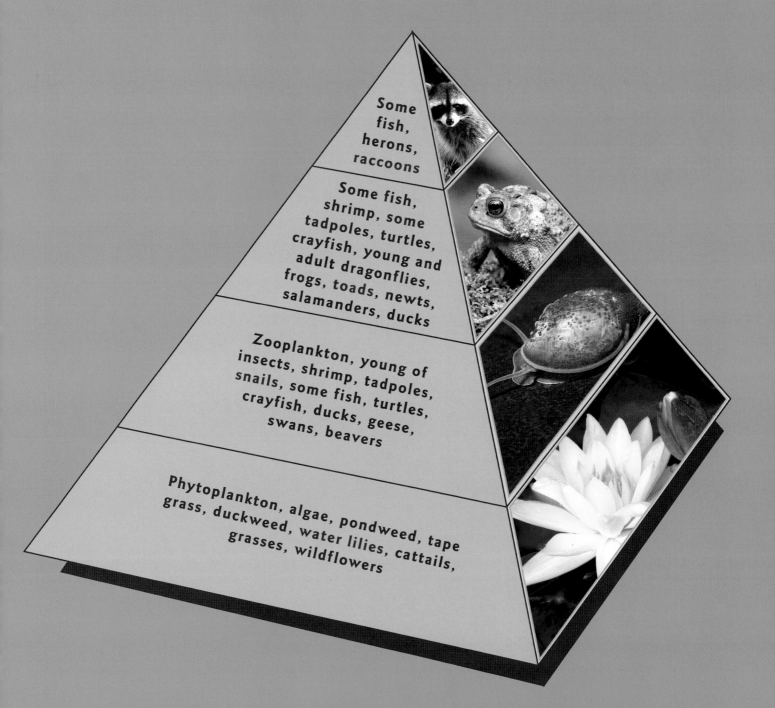

Some fish, herons, raccoons

Some fish, shrimp, some tadpoles, turtles, crayfish, young and adult dragonflies, frogs, toads, newts, salamanders, ducks

Zooplankton, young of insects, shrimp, tadpoles, snails, some fish, turtles, crayfish, ducks, geese, swans, beavers

Phytoplankton, algae, pondweed, tape grass, duckweed, water lilies, cattails, grasses, wildflowers

TAKING CARE OF POND HABITATS

Pond habitats are important! We must take care of them. Never throw trash into a pond. Trash **pollutes** the pond and hurts plants and animals.

Do not bring strange plants or animals into a pond habitat. Strange plants may crowd out other plants that grow there. Animals that eat the old plants will not have food. Strange animals may eat too many plants or crowd out other animals. This hurts the habitat.

Can you think of other ways to keep ponds healthy? Use what you have learned about graphic organizers to make one showing ways to care for pond habitats!

GLOSSARY

crustaceans (krus-TAY-shunz) Animals that have no backbones, have hard shells, and live mostly in water.

gills (GILZ) Body parts that fish use for breathing.

glaciers (GLAY-shurz) Large masses of ice that move down a mountain or along a valley.

insects (IN-sekts) Small creatures that often have six legs and wings.

life cycle (LYF SY-kul) The different periods through which a living thing passes from birth to death.

lungs (LUNGZ) The parts of an air-breathing animal that take in air and supply oxygen to the blood.

oxygen (OK-sih-jen) A gas that has no color or taste and is necessary for people and animals to breathe.

phytoplankton (fy-toh-PLANK-tun) Ocean plant life made up of one cell.

pollutes (puh-LOOTS) Hurts with bad matter.

submersed (sub-MERSD) Covered by water.

tadpoles (TAD-pohlz) Baby frogs or toads that look like fish and live under the water.

zooplankton (zoh-uh-PLANK-tun) Tiny animals that float freely in water.

INDEX

WEB SITES

Due to the changing nature of Internet links, PowerKids
Press has developed an online list of Web sites related
to the subject of this book. This site is updated regularly.
Please use this link to access the list:
www.powerkidslinks.com/graphoh/pond/